Praise for *Selling in the Paddock*

'Georgia has a rare talent for simplifying the human side of ag sales. She gets the industry, understands people, and knows exactly how to help sales teams communicate with purpose instead of noise. Her work is practical, honest and grounded in real-world experience—not just theory.

I see the capability gaps across ag every day, and what Georgia coaches is what so many businesses are crying out for. She gives people confidence, clarity and a framework that actually works in the field.

If you want to lift your game, build stronger relationships and deliver real value to customers, this book should be at the top of your list.'

KELLI MCDOUGALL, managing director, Agri Talent and Global People Solutions

'I'd been trying to crack into a client for eighteen months and was giving him everything—trial data, product features, technical details—but couldn't get the time of day. After doing Georgia's DISC workshop, the lightbulb went on. He was a high-D personality, and all he really wanted to know was three things: does it work, does it make me money, and is it easy to use? So I went back with exactly that message—plus proof that another local producer was getting an extra $80 a head from reduced dark cutting. I left him a drum with a simple offer: if it didn't deliver results at the processor, I'd credit it. It worked. He used it for a long time after. Georgia's training genuinely changed the way I sell.'

CHRIS BOSTON, state farm supplies manager SA/Sunraysia, Elders

'Georgia is the perfect example of what relationship building and trust looks like in agriculture. One conversation with Georgia and it's hard not to feel her authentic care in listening to you as a human.

Selling in the Paddock *reflects real life agriculture and how it looks and feels in Australia—long days, tough conversations, and relationships that matter more than ruthless sales strategy.*

This book will resonate strongly with sales professionals, leaders and business owners because it's practical and grounded in her lived experience in Australian agriculture.

In ag sales, it is extremely rare to meet someone who, from the first conversation, makes you feel like you've known them for years. That's what you get with Georgia.'

MARK ALLOTT, national sales manager, Kubota

'Selling in the Paddock *is a must-read for anyone selling in agriculture, from frontline salespeople to sales leaders. It's a practical, no-nonsense playbook that focuses on what truly drives results: people buy from people.*

Georgia shows how to build trust, communicate with clarity, handle challenges with integrity and close with confidence. Real, relevant and highly actionable, this book equips agri-sales professionals and sales leaders to be exceptional at what they do, every single day.'

DARREN MITCHELL, sales leadership coach and host of *The Exceptional Sales Leader* podcast

Selling in the Paddock

Selling in the Paddock

A proven, people-first framework for selling with confidence in agriculture

GEORGIA STORMONT

Published by Grammar Factory Publishing, an imprint of MacMillan Company Limited.

Grammar Factory Publishing
MacMillan Company Limited
25 Telegram Mews, 39th Floor, Suite 3906
Toronto, Ontario, Canada
M5V 3Z1

www.grammarfactory.com

Stormont, Georgia.
Selling in the Paddock: A proven, people-first framework for selling with confidence in agriculture / Georgia Stormont.

Paperback ISBN 978-1-998528-81-3
eBook ISBN 978-1-998528-82-0

1. BUS021000 BUSINESS & ECONOMICS / Sales & Selling / General.
2. BUS043000 BUSINESS & ECONOMICS / Industries / Agribusiness.
3. BUS025000 BUSINESS & ECONOMICS / Entrepreneurship.

Production Credits
Cover design by Designerbility
Interior layout design by Setareh Ashrafologhalai
Book production and editorial services by Grammar Factory Publishing

Grammar Factory's Carbon Neutral Publishing Commitment
Grammar Factory Publishing is proud to be neutralising the carbon footprint of all printed copies of its authors' books printed by or ordered directly through Grammar Factory or its affiliated companies through the purchase of Gold Standard-Certified International Offsets.

For Mum and Dad
You backed me when my thinking
didn't fit the mould—you saw
strength when others saw disruption.

For Daniel, Rosie, Noah and Ada
Thank you for your patience,
encouragement and unwavering
support in bringing this book to life.

CONTENTS

FOREWORD

I'VE KNOWN GEORGIA STORMONT for well over a decade, going right back to her days as a sales rep. She was calling on our farms in Tasmania, and even then it was obvious she wasn't your average sales rep. Georgia had a rare mix of technical knowledge, commercial awareness and genuine curiosity about how our operation worked. Most importantly, she knew how to talk to growers—not at us, but with us.

When Georgia started her own business, I asked her to come and consult with us. You don't offer that sort of invitation unless someone has made a real impression. Since then, she has continued working closely with our industry through Tasman Seeds, a business Harvest Moon is a major shareholder in. Georgia now sells onion seed for our company around Australia, and she has always represented the business with the same integrity, energy and professionalism she showed from day one.

That ongoing relationship has only reinforced my view: Georgia understands farming, she understands people, and she understands what real selling looks like in agriculture.

Our industry is a tough one. We deal with weather, labour, markets, risk, timing and constant pressure. Good salespeople in ag know this. They understand that growers value competence, clarity and trust—not flash presentations or empty promises. Georgia has always stood out because she communicates honestly, listens properly, and brings practical solutions that respect how farmers think and what they need.

This book reflects all of that.

Selling in the Paddock is not a corporate textbook. It's a practical guide for anyone selling into agriculture—agronomists, seed reps, merchandisers, territory managers, sales leaders. Georgia has taken the lessons she's lived—the conversations at the back of utes, the early-morning paddock visits, the tough seasons and tight markets—and turned them into a framework that genuinely helps people do their job better.

What I respect most is that Georgia has never lost sight of the grower. Everything she teaches comes back to building real relationships and communicating in a way that earns trust. That's why this book matters. It shows the next generation of ag sales professionals what works, why it works, and how to bring more confidence and integrity into every interaction.

I'm proud to write this foreword, and even prouder to see someone with Georgia's experience and character put these lessons into a book that will help strengthen our industry for years to come.

MARK KABLE
Managing director and CEO
Harvest Moon/Tasman Seeds

INTRODUCTION
WELCOME TO THE PADDOCK

I DIDN'T GROW up on a farm.

When I first stepped into agriculture, I was the city kid with clean boots and a notepad full of questions. I learnt quickly that selling in ag isn't about slick pitches or shiny presentations—it's about people. Real people. People who live where they work, who make decisions that affect their land, their families and their future.

Over the past fifteen years, I've sat at kitchen tables, climbed into tractors, walked countless rows, and stood in more paddocks than I can remember. I've worked alongside dairy farmers, sold seed and now coach people selling into ag.

And I've noticed something.

Most people in ag don't see themselves as 'salespeople'. They see themselves as problem solvers, helpers, relationship builders—caretakers of something bigger. That's why selling often feels uncomfortable. Even unnatural.

Maybe you've felt it too...

You know your product is good, but freeze when it's time to ask for the order.

You want to help growers, not push them—but worry you'll come across the wrong way.

You spend hours building relationships, only to feel unheard when it counts.

You can explain the agronomy perfectly, but struggle to influence decisions.

You leave meetings thinking, 'They like me... so why didn't they buy?'

Selling in agriculture is hard—even for the people who look like naturals.

Why? Because you're not just selling a product. You're selling trust first. Everything else follows.

And when trust is the product, doubt becomes the barrier.

Let me show you.

A story from the paddock

A few years ago, I drove up a long driveway to see a grower in northern Tasmania. We've all felt that moment—the mix of nerves and anticipation as you pull up, take a deep breath and walk towards the front door.

He listened politely. Asked good questions. Smiled. Nodded. Said, 'Yeah, looks good. Leave it with me.'

And then nothing.

Days passed. Then weeks. Then months.

I replayed the meeting in my head. *Did I talk too much? Not enough? Should I have closed more directly? Should I have held back?*

What I learnt later was this:

He wasn't unsure about the product. He was unsure about *me*.

Not because I'd done anything wrong—but because growers have been burnt before. They've seen reps vanish after the sale. They've trialled products that didn't perform. They've heard promises that didn't match reality.

So they go slow. They wait. They protect themselves.

And that hesitation—that silent space between interest and action—is where most sales fall over.

Not because of price. Not because of yield. But because trust wasn't built deeply enough, early enough.

Who I am—and why I'm here

I've been selling in agriculture for more than fifteen years—but I didn't start in horticulture or sales coaching. I started in dairy.

I've milked plenty of cows at 4 am. I've stood in muddy dairy yards, learning the pace and rhythm of farm life. I've driven up countless farm tracks and driveways, not knowing who or what would be waiting at the other end. I've sat at kitchen tables, boots dripping on the mat, listening to what really matters to farmers.

Over the years, my work has taken me from dairy to horticulture to national sales teams across Australia. I've sold vegetable seed, run trials, worked with global suppliers, and supported growers through droughts, floods, gluts, shortages and everything in between.

I've spoken at national conferences, coached sales teams across Australia, and helped agricultural businesses improve both confidence and commercial outcomes.

I've been the rep in the ute doing 60,000 km a year—exhausted, hopeful and learning on the fly. And now I'm the coach who helps agricultural teams build confidence, communicate better, and sell in a way that feels natural rather than forced.

Across all of that, one thing has stayed constant:

Agriculture deserves better sales training—training built for the paddock, not borrowed from corporate textbooks.

That's why I wrote this book.

To give people in ag a framework that actually works in real conversations, with real growers, in real seasons—without the bullshit, without the pressure, and without trying to turn good people into something they're not. Today, the Selling in the Paddock™ framework is used by agricultural sales teams across Australia to improve conversations, confidence and results.

Selling in the Paddock Blueprint™

Confidence in Sales doesn't come from scripts or gimmicks. It comes from knowing who you are, reading the room, handling the hard bits, and driving it home.

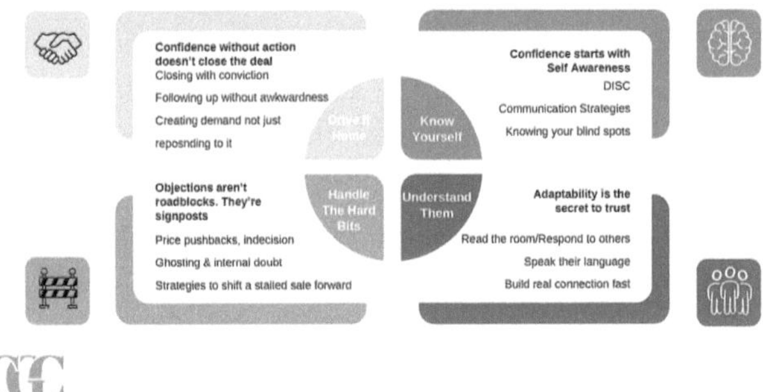

The Selling in the Paddock™ framework

This book follows the four-part framework I use when coaching sales teams across Australia. It's simple, practical and human—and it works.

Part 1: Know Yourself

Before you can influence someone else, you need to understand your own wiring. Your pace. Your reactions. Your fears. Your strengths.

Benefits of knowing yourself:

- You become clearer, calmer and more grounded.
- You hesitate less.
- Your confidence becomes real, not 'fake it 'til you make it'.

Risks of not knowing yourself:

- You take things personally.
- You react instead of responding.
- You shrink when pressure hits.

Part 2: Understand Others

Sales isn't a solo sport—it's a conversation. Different people buy differently. Different personalities need different approaches.

Benefits of understanding others:

- You build trust faster.
- You adapt easily.
- You stop losing deals purely from mismatched communication.

Risks of not understanding others:

- You come across as pushy or vague without meaning to.
- You miss the cues buyers are giving you.
- You lose opportunities that were yours to win.

Part 3: Handle the Hard Bits

Pressure is a given in ag. Objections, seasons, budgets, competition, fatigue—they're all part of the job.

Benefits of handling the hard bits:

- You stay calm when others panic.
- You navigate objections with confidence and care.
- Your reputation strengthens because you hold your nerve.

Risks of not handling the hard bits:

- You avoid tough conversations.
- You crumble under pressure.
- You lose respect—and sales.

Part 4: Drive It Home

This is where courage becomes action. Closing isn't force—it's clarity.

Benefits of driving it home:

- You stop leaving sales 'almost done'.
- You close more with less stress.
- Buyers feel supported, not pushed.

Risks of not driving it home:

- You do ninety per cent of the work but never finish the conversation.
- Your confidence erodes.
- Buyers walk away unclear—and unclear buyers don't buy.

What this book will give you

You'll walk away with:

- A deeper understanding of yourself
- The ability to read others quickly
- Tools to handle objections and pressure
- Confidence to close conversations clearly
- Real-world examples, scripts and stories
- A framework that feels natural, practical and human

Ultimately, you'll learn to sell in a way that feels like *you.*

That's the heart of this book.
Helping you find your voice, own your value, and lead conversations that move people—in any paddock, branch or boardroom.

Welcome to the paddock. Let's get started.

PART 1

KNOW YOURSELF

BEFORE WE TALK about clients, conversations or conversions, we have to start with you.

Not the version of you with the brochure and the sales target. The real you. The one behind the wheel on a long paddock drive, who sometimes wonders if you're getting it right.

Knowing yourself is the foundation of everything else—your resilience, your influence, your ability to lead and listen.

And to show what that looks like under pressure, we're not starting in a paddock at all. We're starting in Antarctica.

Leadership when everything breaks

In 1914, explorer Ernest Shackleton set out on an expedition to cross Antarctica on foot—a feat no one had achieved. He and his crew of twenty-seven boarded the *Endurance* and headed towards the South Pole, filled with ambition, scientific curiosity and hope.

They never made it.

Just months after arriving in the Weddell Sea, the *Endurance* became trapped in pack ice. For ten months, it was crushed slowly until it sank—leaving the crew stranded on shifting ice floes with no shelter, no radio, and no way to call for help. Temperatures dropped to -40 °C. Supplies dwindled. Morale wavered.

And here's where the story shifts—not into tragedy, but into extraordinary leadership.

For nearly two years, Shackleton kept every single man alive. Not one crew member died. He made brutal decisions with calm clarity. He sacrificed his own safety to save others. And he maintained discipline—and dignity—even when hope seemed lost.

How?

He knew himself.

Shackleton's journals reveal a man who deeply understood his own fears, his limits and the weight of his leadership. He once wrote: *'Difficulties are just things to overcome, after all.'*

But he didn't ignore emotion. He felt it. Sat with it. Used it to fuel empathy.

He recognised that the real enemy wasn't the cold or the hunger. It was despair. And if he cracked, the crew would too. So he played the role they needed: unshakeable, forward-looking, deeply human. He kept spirits up with routine. Encouraged singing. Held back bad news when timing mattered. Knew when to push—and when to pause.

In one critical moment, when a crew member panicked during a trek across the ice, Shackleton didn't yell or shame him. He quietly took the man's hand, steadied him, and walked in silence until he calmed. No fanfare. Just presence.

This wasn't the loud, charismatic leadership of a hero's tale. It was self-aware, grounded and intentional. Shackleton knew who he was—and what his team needed him to be.

What this means for ag sales

You may not be stranded on Antarctic ice, but some seasons of this job feel just as isolating. A drought hits. A grower pulls a contract. You drive five hours to be told, 'Not interested.'

In those moments, knowing yourself is everything.

- What triggers you?
- What settles you?
- What do you default to when pressure hits? Control? Avoidance? Overtalking?

Shackleton didn't survive because he was fearless. He survived because he was honest—about who he was, what he felt, and what was needed in the moment.

And he led from that place.

KEY TAKEAWAY

You can't lead others—or sell with authenticity—until you lead yourself. Know your fear. Know your strength. And show up, even when it's hard.

It all starts in your own paddock—with confidence, clarity and courage before the call.

Before you can sell to anyone else, you have to understand yourself.

The best salespeople in agriculture aren't the loudest or the flashiest; they're the ones who know who they are, how they communicate and how to steady themselves when things get hard.

This part is about that inner paddock—the space between your ears and in your chest. Because when you get that right, everything else grows from there.

1

TAKING THE LEAP

EVERY SALESPERSON KNOWS that moment—the one just before you do something uncomfortable. The long walk up a driveway. The pause before you make a call you've been putting off. The breath you take before asking a tough question or stepping into a room full of experience.

Courage never feels calm in the beginning. It feels shaky, loud and a bit ridiculous. But it's also the doorway to confidence—and that's what this chapter is about.

Before we get into tools, techniques and frameworks, we need to start with the foundation that sits underneath every great conversation in agriculture: your ability to act even when you don't feel ready.

And nothing taught me that lesson more clearly than the day I jumped off a bridge in Queenstown.

The morning of

The morning of the jump, I woke up in the hotel room and immediately thought, *What the hell am I doing?*

The curtains were half open, the mountains still blue with early light, and my stomach already felt like it was free-falling. I'd booked this bungee during our sales meeting—a burst of 'practise what you preach' energy. I tell people every day to step beyond their comfort zone, and now here I was, terrified of heights, wishing I'd chosen the wine tour.

I called Daniel and the kids that morning but didn't mention it. I couldn't. Saying it out loud would've made it too real.

Downstairs, I met Josh—my colleague and unofficial emotional-support person. He looked maddeningly calm, coffee in hand, cracking jokes while we signed the waivers. Then the weigh-in. I laughed nervously, thinking, *Great, now they know exactly how heavy I'll fall.*

The bus ride up was where it really hit me. The windows fogged with our breath as Queenstown blurred by in shades of green and grey. Josh kept chatting—dinner last night, the view, the playlist—and that helped. I told him, 'I'm shitting myself.' He laughed and said, 'We're in this together. You'll be okay.'

At the top it was cold enough to bite. We checked in, paid for the video—*of course* I needed proof, something to show myself one day when I'm old and forgetful that I really did this. Then came the crew: straps, harnesses, cheerful instructions. My name ticked off a clipboard, my legs bound like a cartoon character's.

I walked onto the platform, the river carving through the valley below, and leaned just far enough over the rail to feel the drop pull at my stomach. That was the line—the point where you can't back away without regretting it forever.

The jump

The crew called my name. Harness checked. Ankles strapped. Thumbs-up all around.

Then they picked up the rope.

Until that moment it had just been an idea—something I could still laugh off—but when they started feeding the cord over the railing, I heard it hiss and drag against the steel. It was *heavy.* The kind of heavy that says, *There's no turning back now.*

I felt the pull through my legs as they clipped it on and held me steady at the edge. One of the crew grinned and said, 'Don't worry, we've got you.'

I remember thinking, *If they let go, I'm gone.*

The rope coiled and swung between us like a living thing. Every instinct screamed, *Step back,* but another voice—quieter, steadier—said, *You've done scarier things. You just don't call them that.*

'Ready?'

'Yep,' I lied.

I didn't look down. I took one slow breath, stretched my arms out like I was on the bow of the *Titanic,* and leaned forward.

Then I went.

What came out wasn't a brave yell—it was a full-bodied, murderous scream. The wind punched the sound right out of me. Then . . . nothing.

Silence. A strange, weightless calm in the middle of chaos.

For maybe five seconds—though it felt like a lifetime—time slowed down. I could think. I could *feel* everything: the rush of air, the sting of cold on my cheeks, the deep quiet of doing something that terrified me.

Then the cord reached its max. A sharp pull, a snap of gravity, and I shot back up, laughing and crying all at once.

Confidence didn't come before courage; it arrived on the rebound.

The realisation

When the cord finally stilled, I hung there upside down, still laughing and crying at the same time. The world spun slowly—sky, river, cliffs—and I couldn't stop smiling.

Below me, two crew waited in a small inflatable boat. One called out, 'Grab the pole when you swing towards us!'

I reached, missed, reached again, caught it. They hauled me in, still laughing.

'Did you see me, Josh?!' I yelled up towards the bridge.

He was leaning over the railing, both arms in the air, cheering like a proud coach. I must've sounded like a kid—or Sally Pearson in that post-race interview—breathless, high on relief, grinning like an idiot.

They unclipped me, and suddenly I was free again—sitting in the bottom of the boat, heart pounding, adrenaline buzzing.

That's when it hit me: This wasn't about conquering heights. It was about recognising the pattern.

That surge of fear before the jump is the same feeling that shows up before every big move—before calling a new client, walking up a long farm driveway, or pitching a new idea.

The bridge might've been higher, the stakes different, but the story underneath was the same. Courage always comes first. Confidence follows.

The lesson

Back on solid ground, my legs were still trembling—not from cold, but from pure adrenaline. I hadn't touched the river; I'd hung just above it, suspended in mid-air, watching the world swing beneath me.

It wasn't the view that stayed with me. It was that moment—the space between *ready* and *go.*

That fear shows up everywhere. Fear is just the brain trying to keep you safe. Courage is the part of you that moves anyway.

When we take that step—make the call, say the thing, start the conversation—our brain rewards the action. Dopamine and endorphins flood in, proving we're capable. That's why fear fades the moment you move.

Most people wait to feel confident before they act, but confidence is the outcome, not the entry ticket.

Courage fires first. Confidence follows.

And courage isn't recklessness. It's not blind risk; it's choosing to move forward with preparation and purpose—knowing the rope's secure even if your stomach isn't.

In agriculture, courage looks quieter but feels the same:

- The rep making a cold call after a tough season,
- The grower trialling something new, or
- The young agronomist speaking up in a room full of experience.

They're all standing on their own bridge—heart racing, rope heavy—and choosing to jump anyway. So when fear shows up before your next big step, remember: That's proof you're at the edge of growth. Take one breath. Trust the rope. And jump. Because the magic never happens while you're still on the platform.

Podcast wisdom

Over the years, I've interviewed dozens of people on the *Selling in the Paddock* podcast—growers, leaders, negotiators, livestock agents and incredible thinkers in agriculture. Their stories and lessons often deepen the ideas in this book, and this is one of those moments.

Rural property and livestock agent Jimmy Blain summed it up perfectly:

> *'Put yourself in situations that feel a bit daunting and test yourself. The more pressure you expose yourself to, the less scary it gets.'*

Jimmy wasn't talking about bungee jumping—he was talking about life in ag. Every auction, every negotiation, every tough conversation with a grower is its own edge. Courage builds capacity.

A few episodes later, Paul Roos, AFL premiership coach and leadership icon, said something that ties it all together:

> *'Calm isn't weakness—it's strength under control. When you know what you stand for, the noise fades.'*

The calm doesn't come before the chaos—it arrives once you're already in it. That's the real gift of courage: The moment you leap, fear loses its grip.

REFLECTION AND ACTION

Before you move on, take a moment to step out of my story and into your own. Courage looks different for everyone in agriculture—but the feeling underneath is the same. Use this space to recognise where fear shows up in your work and where a small, brave step could shift everything. Ask yourself:

- What's your 'bungee jump'?
- If you were brave enough, what's one leap you'd take this week?

2

DISC IN THE PADDOCK

SOME OF THE TOUGHEST moments in sales come from conversations that just don't land. You're speaking clearly, the information is solid, the product makes sense—and yet something feels off. The pace is wrong, the energy is mismatched, or the connection just isn't there.

This chapter is about understanding why.

The biggest shift in my own sales career happened when I stopped assuming everyone communicated like me. Once I learnt how to read people better—their pace, their style, their decision-making clues—conversations became smoother. Not easier in the sense of less effort, but easier because I stopped fighting the wrong battles.

Let me show you how this plays out in the paddock.

The Gippsland growers: fast talker vs deep thinker

Years ago, I visited two growers on a single day in Gippsland. Same region. Same day. Same product. Completely different worlds.

The first grower was what I call a **fast talker**. Before my boots even hit the ground, he was firing questions at me:

'Right, what've you got? What's the price? How soon can I get it? Show me the trial data.'

I had to lift my energy and meet him where he was—quick, direct, sharp. No fluff. No stories. The entire conversation was done in under ten minutes and he made a decision on the spot.

Then I headed to the second grower—the **deep thinker**.

This farmer moved at a much slower pace. He listened. Paused. Considered. His questions were thoughtful, not rapid-fire. He wasn't being difficult—he just needed time. Space. Certainty.

If I'd used the same high-speed approach I used with the first grower, he would've quietly shut down. Not because the product was wrong—but because the approach would've been wrong *for him*.

That's when I realised:

It's not about the product. It's about the person.

The way they communicate. The way they process information. The way they build trust.

That's where DISC comes in.

What DISC really means in agriculture

DISC, which is an acronym for **D**ominance, **I**nfluence, **S**teadiness, **C**onscientiousness (more on this in a moment), is a tool to help you recognise communication patterns—not personality 'types'.

In agriculture, it's pure gold because conversations aren't happening in corporate meeting rooms. They're happening:

- In paddocks,
- In sheds,
- In mud,
- Beside utes,
- On the move, and
- In moments where time, seasons and pressure matter.

Growers don't have time for long-winded explanations. They don't want to be lectured. They don't want pressure. But they do want to feel understood.

DISC helps you get there faster.

DISC quick reference guide
(Designed specifically for ag conversations)

STYLE	WHAT THEY VALUE	COMMUNICATION STYLE	CLUES TO LOOK FOR	HOW TO SELL TO THEM
D— Driver (Decisive)	Action, results, speed	Fast, direct, blunt	Little small talk, short sentences, quick decisions	Be brief, remain confident, and lead with outcomes. Don't waffle.
I— Influencer (People-first)	Connection, energy	Expressive, warm, story-driven	Animated tone, big gestures	Build rapport first. Use stories and enthusiasm.
S— Steady (Supportive)	Safety, consistency	Calm, gentle, paced	Soft tone, avoids conflict	Slow down. Reassure. Show reliability and ongoing support.
C— Conscientious (Analytical)	Accuracy, detail	Measured, logical	Asks technical questions, wants data	Bring proof, trials, comparisons. Don't guess or wing it.

How to apply DISC in real conversations

You don't need to guess someone's DISC style. You just need to pay attention.

A simple rule:

If they speed up, you speed up. If they slow down, you slow down.

Because here's the truth:

- A **Driver** hears confidence through clarity and brevity.
- An **Influencer** hears confidence through warmth and connection.
- A **Steady** operator hears confidence through patience and reassurance.
- A **Conscientious** thinker hears confidence through data and preparedness.

When you flex slightly towards someone else's style, you're not being 'fake'. You're being **effective**.

On the *Selling in the Paddock* podcast, emotional intelligence expert Nathan Jones shared something that perfectly ties into DISC:

> *'All emotions belong. When you learn to read the signals—yours and someone else's—influence becomes natural.'*

That's what DISC helps you do: read signals quickly, adjust early and build trust without force.

REFLECTION AND ACTION

DISC helps you communicate in a way people can actually hear. When you match pace, adjust style and honour how others decide, everything becomes easier—conversations, relationships and sales. Take a moment to think about three growers or customers you've visited in the last month. Ask yourself:

- Which DISC style did each one lean towards?
- Where could you have adjusted your pace, tone or level of detail to better match them?

3

FINDING FLOW IN SALES

SOME DAYS IN sales feel effortless. The conversations land, the questions flow, the energy is good, and buyers seem open, relaxed and willing. Other days feel clunky, disjointed and hard, no matter how much effort you throw at them. This chapter is about understanding why. Finding flow in sales isn't down to luck—it's about awareness. When you know how to regulate your own energy, read the moment in front of you and match the pace of the person you're speaking with, everything becomes smoother.

This chapter will help you recognise what throws you off, what brings you back, and how to create more of those days where everything just works.

The out-of-flow day

The day started wrong and kept getting worse.

I'd left the house late, realised halfway down the highway I'd forgotten the trial samples, and my phone battery was already in the red. By the time I pulled into the first farm gate, I was flustered, hungry, and about three coffees short of human.

The grower was waiting, polite but impatient. I rushed through my pitch, stumbled over the data and felt myself talking faster—trying to make up for lost ground. His expression didn't change. Somewhere between the third stat and the awkward laugh, I knew I'd lost him.

As I drove away, I muttered something to myself that can't be printed and slapped the steering wheel. The paddocks rolled by, perfect rows under a perfect sky, and all I could think was, *This isn't me. Where the hell is my rhythm today?*

I wasn't in flow. I was forcing it. And in sales—just like in farming—forcing rarely ends well.

The good day

A few days later, the rhythm came back.

Same car, same roads, same me—but everything just *worked*.

I'd left on time, playlist humming, phone charged, route mapped. The morning sun hit the paddocks just right—that golden light that makes you remember why you love this job.

The first grower visit was easy. We laughed, walked the rows, talked about the crop, and sorted an order without a single awkward pause. The next stop, the merch manager waved me straight through—'You're on fire today, Georgia.'

Every conversation seemed to flow into the next. No push, no panic, no forcing. Just clean rhythm. I knew what to say and when to stop talking. The farmers were engaged, asking good questions, actually smiling. Even the coffee at the servo was decent.

Driving between visits, I caught myself smiling for no reason. Not relief, not ego—just that quiet buzz you get when you know you're doing what you're meant to be doing.

By the time I parked the ute that evening, I'd clocked five farm calls, three solid orders, and more genuine conversations than I could count. It didn't feel like work—it felt like flow.

That's the thing about flow—you can't fake it, and you can't force it. It's that sweet spot where preparation meets presence, and the rest just clicks.

I remember thinking, *I could do this forever.*

The realisation

That good day got me thinking. *Why did everything click?* It wasn't luck. The roads were the same, the growers were the same, even the weather wasn't that different. The difference was *me*.

I'd shown up prepared, present, and with a clear purpose. And that, I realised, is what flow really is.

Psychologist Mihály Csíkszentmihályi—who has one of the most impossible names to spell—described flow as the state where you're so absorbed in what you're doing that everything else falls away. Time bends, distractions fade, and you're fully in it.

He said we're hit with about two million bits of information every second, but our brains can only process about 156. Flow is when all 156 are focused in one direction.

And I reckon that's exactly what happens on those great sales days. You're not half-thinking about emails, budgets or what's for dinner. You're just there—tuned in, responsive, and reading the moment like a good stockman reads the mob.

That's the balance between skill and challenge—where you're stretched just enough to stay engaged, but not so far that you panic.

When you're in flow, conversations don't feel like selling—they feel like connection. The words come naturally, your instincts are sharper and you actually *enjoy* the work. And people can feel it too—they lean in because your energy's clean and congruent.

Looking back, that day on the road wasn't about luck or timing. It was about alignment—the right mindset, the right preparation, the right presence.

I hadn't changed what I was doing; I'd changed *how* I was showing up to it.

You can't fake flow. But you can build the conditions for it.

That means setting up your day with intention—not racing from farm to farm, but planning routes that make sense. Knowing your data so you're not fumbling for answers. Giving each person your full attention instead of scanning your phone between conversations.

Because distraction kills flow faster than a flat tyre on a Friday afternoon.

Finding your unique flow

We all experience flow differently. Some people *see* the picture in their head—the layout of the field, the colour of the crop.

Others *hear* the rhythm—the sound of a conversation when it's clicking.

Some *feel* it—that gut sense when the connection's right.

And a few process it through logic and analysis—ticking off the mental checklist as they go.

Those are our communication styles—Visual, Auditory, Kinaesthetic and Audio Digital—and understanding them is the next step to mastering flow in others.

We'll get into that soon. For now, just notice how *you* find your rhythm.

REFLECTION AND ACTION

Flow isn't luck—it's the reward for being prepared, present and purposeful. When you understand your rhythm, the paddock, the people and the sale, all start to move in sync. And that's where the real influence lives—not in the push, but in the flow.

Before your next day on the road or your next big meeting, take five minutes and ask yourself:

- When do I feel most 'in flow'? What does it feel like in my body?
- What tends to pull me *out* of flow—rushing, pressure, distractions?
- What small habits could help me stay more present—before, during and after conversations?
- Do I tend to see, hear, feel or analyse information first?

PART 2

UNDERSTAND OTHERS

F PART 1 helped you understand your own wiring—your pace, your reactions, your triggers and your confidence—then Part 2 is where we turn that awareness outward.

Because here's the truth:

You can know yourself deeply, but, unless you understand the person standing in front of you, sales will always feel harder than they need to be.

When you don't understand others, sales feels like pushing. When you *do* understand others, it feels like connection. Let me give you a real-life example.

Tailor your message

On the night of 18 April 1775, two men set out on horseback from Boston with the same mission: Warn the countryside that British troops were marching.

You've likely heard of one of them—Paul Revere. You've likely never heard of the other—William Dawes.

They rode in opposite directions, covering similar ground, both trying to spark the American militia into action. But while Revere's ride triggered a wave of preparation and mobilised entire towns, Dawes' effort mostly fell flat.

Why? Not because Revere was faster. Not because he yelled louder. But because he knew his audience—and adapted his message accordingly.

Revere was a silversmith by trade, but, more importantly, he was a networker. He belonged to every influential group in Boston—from merchants to mechanics to freemasons. He didn't just deliver a message that night; he delivered *the right message to the right people in the right way*.

When he knocked on a door, he knew who he was talking to. If it was a blacksmith, he spoke in practical terms. If it was a farmer, he appealed to their land and liberty. If it was a community leader, he offered strategy. He used names, not slogans. Questions, not commands.

William Dawes? He was just a guy on a horse with a warning. Revere didn't just yell, 'The British are coming!'—that line's more legend than fact. What he actually did was *tailor* his words to the person in front of him. And they listened.

What this means for ag sales

You can have the best product, the best pitch and the best price—but if you're not speaking your buyer's language, it'll fall flat.

I've seen reps walk into a grower meeting and lead with data, when the grower is driven by gut feel. Or use vague benefit statements like, 'It'll boost performance,' when the customer wants hard numbers. I've done it myself.

Understanding others isn't about tricking or manipulating. It's about **listening first**, reading the room, and showing the person in front of you that you see them. That you *get* them.

And when you do that, trust follows. Decisions follow. Action follows.

KEY TAKEAWAY

Influence doesn't come from how loudly you speak—it comes from how well you listen. If you want your message to land, start by understanding the person you're delivering it to.

Because no two paddocks—or people—grow the same way.

Some need facts and figures.

Some need to feel it in their hands.

Some need time to think.

And some just need to know you see *them*, not just their acreage or account number.

Selling in agriculture is as much about human connection as it is about agronomy or price. The best salespeople don't have the slickest pitch—they have empathy. They read the room, match the moment, and adapt their communication so others can actually hear them.

That's what Part 2 is about. You'll learn how to listen between the lines, build trust that lasts beyond one season, and connect in a way that feels natural—whether you're at a kitchen table, at a branch counter or out in the paddock.

4

BUILDING TRUST WITH THE CAUTIOUS BUYER

EVERY SALESPERSON KNOWS the buyer who sits back a little. The one who listens carefully, asks considered questions, hesitates before making a call, and always needs 'a bit more time' before committing. This chapter is all about *that buyer*—the cautious one.

And here's the key: Caution isn't a lack of interest. Caution is a form of protection.

These buyers want to make the right decision. They want to feel safe with the person in front of them. They don't rush, not because they don't trust you, but because they're trying to understand whether you are someone worth trusting.

Trust comes first. Pitch comes second.

I once spent weeks working with a buyer—let's call him Charles—who was smart, thorough, and thoughtful. He never rushed. He asked good questions. He made notes. He processed quietly. His pace was steady, grounded and very deliberate.

He wasn't cold. He wasn't uninterested. He was cautious. And if you push a cautious buyer, you lose them instantly.

Standing in his packing shed, I remember wanting so badly to speed things up. In my mind, everything was obvious. The trial results were strong, the pricing worked, and he already liked me. But every time I tried to move the conversation forward, he slowed it down.

It wasn't resistance. It was *his process*. He needed to think it through in *his* way, not mine.

That experience taught me something I've seen repeated thousands of times since: **People don't buy when you are ready. They buy when they feel safe.**

The makeup of cautious buyers

Cautious buyers often fall into the S or C styles of DISC:

- S-style (Steady)—calm, loyal, patient, prefers stability
- C-style (Conscientious)—analytical, detail-oriented, values accuracy

These aren't 'slow' buyers. They're *careful* buyers. They want to:

- Understand the risk,
- Understand the plan,
- Understand you, and
- Understand what happens if things go wrong.

They're not buying your product. They're buying their own peace of mind. Nathan Jones, an emotional intelligence specialist I interviewed on the podcast, summed it up perfectly:

> *'Some people buy with emotion and justify with logic. Others start with logic and wait until the emotion catches up.'*

Cautious buyers are in that second group. They need logic first. They need safety first. They need space first. Only then does trust click into place. Once it does, they're incredibly loyal.

VAKAD: how buyers process information

Before we talk about trust and hesitation, it helps to understand *how* people take in information. Not everyone hears, sees or processes the same way. That's where VAKAD comes in:

V = Visual
A = Auditory
K = Kinaesthetic
AD = Audio Digital

It's a communication framework that explains the different ways people absorb and make sense of information.

Your buyer is filtering everything you say—and they're filtering it through *their* preferred channel. When you understand the channel they naturally use, you can deliver the information in a way they're most likely to trust, remember and act on.

Let's break down each one.

Visual processors

Visual processors understand through seeing. They prefer:

- Maps, diagrams and photos
- Charts or side-by-side comparisons
- Seeing the paddock or crop themselves

They often say things like:

- 'Show me what you mean.'
- 'What does it look like on-farm?'
- 'Do you have a picture or map of it?'

How to sell to them:

- Bring photos or trial visuals
- Sketch or draw out your point

- Use visual anchor words ('Look at this section...')
- Walk the block with them and physically point things out

Auditory processors

Auditory processors understand through hearing. They pay attention to:

- Tone
- Clarity
- Storytelling
- Verbal structure

They'll say:

- 'Talk me through it.'
- 'Say that again.'
- 'I need to hear the logic.'

How to sell to them:

- Speak calmly and clearly
- Use step-by-step explanations
- Repeat important points
- Use verbal structure ('There are three key things to know...')

Kinaesthetic processors

Kinaesthetic processors understand through doing and feeling. They want:

- Movement
- Experience
- Touch

They say things like:

- 'I want to get my hands on it.'
- 'I need to get a feel for it.'
- 'Let's walk it.'

How to sell to them:

- Walk the paddock together
- Use physical examples ('Feel the soil difference here…')
- Slow down and match their pace
- Allow pauses and space—they process through movement

Audio Digital processors understand through logic, structure and internal reasoning. They rely on:

- Data
- Analysis
- Frameworks
- Comparisons

And they'll say:

- 'Let me think about it.'
- 'Does this add up?'
- 'Walk me through the steps.'

How to sell to them:

- Bring up data, trials and logic
- Provide structure ('Here's the process…')
- Avoid emotional language
- Give them time to think—don't rush the decision

How to use VAKAD in real sales conversations

We're not using VAKAD to label people—we're using it to support them. It's a tool that helps reduce friction and increase clarity, especially with buyers who are thoughtful, deliberate, or slow to make decisions.

Here's how to adjust your approach:

- With a Visual buyer: show, point, draw or walk them through something they can see.
- With an Auditory buyer: explain clearly, be mindful of your tone, verbalise the roadmap.
- With a Kinaesthetic buyer: move with them, walk the paddock, demonstrate physically.
- With an Audio Digital buyer: use logic, numbers and structure—and leave space for thinking.

When someone is taking their time, communicating in their processing style helps them feel understood, safe, clear and confident. And confident buyers make better, faster decisions.

How do you support a cautious buyer?

Trust isn't built in a big moment. It's built, as researcher and author Brené Brown teaches, in the *small moments*—the micro-behaviours that signal:

- 'You're safe.'
- 'I'm listening.'
- 'You can take your time.'
- 'I'm not going anywhere.'
- 'I care about this conversation as much as you do.'

In agriculture, those small behaviours matter more than anything. This includes:

- The way you show up
- The way you wait
- The way you listen
- The way you don't rush
- The way you respect the silence
- The way your body language softens instead of tightens

Before someone trusts your pitch, they have to trust *you*. One of the simplest truths in sales is: People judge your intent before your information.

Darren Wood is the ANZ commercial lead for the vegetable division at Bayer Crop Science, where he works closely with sales teams, growers and commercial partners across the region. With deep experience in complex, high-stakes agricultural environments, Darren understands what real confidence looks like in the paddock and the boardroom alike—not bravado, but clarity, alignment and trust built over time. When he talks about confidence, it comes from seeing firsthand how message, tone and timing directly influence long-term relationships and commercial outcomes.

Darren shared something with me that captures this beautifully:

> *'Confidence isn't volume. It's congruence. People trust you when your message, your tone and your timing all line up.'*

With cautious buyers, congruence matters even more. So, how do you support a cautious buyer—without pushing?

Here are the key points to remember:

1. **Match their pace**. If they're slow, you slow down. If they need reflection time, give it.
2. **Bring detail, not hype**. C-style buyers don't want grand statements. They want data, trials and clarity.
3. **Create safety, not pressure**. Pressure breaks trust. Patience builds it.
4. **Check understanding, not agreement**. Ask: 'Does this make sense so far?' Not: 'So are we ready to go ahead?'
5. **Let silence be silence**. It's not awkward. It's processing.
6. **Finish with clarity**. Give them a simple next step—not a long, open-ended conversation. For example: 'How about I leave this with you and check back in on Thursday?'

REFLECTION AND ACTION

Cautious buyers aren't difficult—they're thoughtful. When you build trust early and support their decision-making process, they become some of your most loyal, long-term customers. Trust first. Pitch second. Always.

Think of a cautious buyer you've worked with recently. Ask yourself:

- Where did you speed up when should you have slowed down?
- Where could you have created more safety, more space or more clarity?

5

SPOTTING AND FLEXING TO COMMUNICATION STYLES

KNOWING THE THEORY behind communication styles is one thing. Putting it into practice—in a paddock, a busy shed, a store or a high-pressure conversation—is something else entirely. This chapter shows you how these styles play out in real sales situations, and how small adjustments in your pace, language and presence can completely shift the outcome. Once you start recognising these patterns in action, you'll communicate with more ease, confidence and influence—no matter who's standing in front of you.

Lost in translation

It was a Monday morning sales meeting, and I was buzzing.

I'd been thinking for weeks about how we could grow the product development side of the business—more trials, new crops, new breeder relationships. It was one of those ideas that had been looping in my head during long drives and late-night note sessions, and I finally couldn't hold it in any longer.

When it came to my turn to share, I launched right in. I started talking—fast, excited, full of energy—about how we could expand into new segments, trial different varieties, explore new partnerships. I was in flow, or at least I thought I was.

But as I spoke, the room went quiet. No nods. No spark. Just polite faces, and blank stares. I remember looking around, thinking, *They don't get it. They don't get me.*

I wrapped it up awkwardly and sat down, my heart racing. Someone else spoke next—presenting a calm, methodical idea, full of data, clear steps, spreadsheets.

And suddenly, everyone leaned in. I sat there, deflated. *Why do they always take on everyone else's ideas? Why not mine?*

For a while, I told myself it was because I was different. I was the creative one. The big-picture thinker. The one who brought the spark.

But over time, I realised that wasn't the problem. It wasn't the idea—it was the *delivery*. I'd been speaking pure Auditory—fast, animated, full of rhythm and feeling—to a room full of Visuals, Audio Digitals and Kinaesthetics.

The Visuals wanted to *see* the idea—diagrams, a roadmap, or even a quick sketch of how it would look. The Audio Digitals wanted it to *make sense*—data, structure, timelines, proof. And the Kinaesthetics wanted to *feel* it—to see how it would land, who it would involve, and how it would change the way we worked day-to-day.

They couldn't visualise what I was saying because I hadn't shown them anything. No facts. No numbers. No diagrams. Just words. So while I was hearing music in my head, they were just hearing noise.

That was the moment it clicked: I wasn't being ignored. I was being lost in translation.

Once I saw that, everything about how I shared ideas changed. I stopped walking into meetings expecting people to hear me the way I *heard myself*. And I started asking: *How do they need to receive it?*

Spotting styles in the wild

Once I realised that my big Monday morning idea had fallen flat not because it was bad, but because I'd spoken the wrong *language*, I started paying attention.

Every conversation became a bit of a detective game. How were people communicating? What words were they using? How quickly were they processing information?

The longer I watched, the clearer the patterns became.

Visual communicators talk in pictures. You'll hear them say things like:

'I can *see* where you're going with this.'

'Can you *show* me what that looks like?'

They crave clarity—whiteboards, photos, maps, graphs. In the paddock, they'll crouch down, studying the leaf colour or plant spacing. In a meeting, they'll reach for the marker or sketch out ideas on paper. If you want to connect with a Visual, paint the picture. Use language like *see, look, imagine, watch.*

Auditory communicators connect through tone and rhythm. They're the ones who say:

'That *sounds* right.'

'*Talk* me through it again.'

You can pick them because they tilt their head slightly when they listen, nod in rhythm with your words, and often replay your points back to you out loud. In agriculture, they're the reps and growers who want to *talk it through on the phone* or while walking rows side by side. They trust what they hear—and *how* they hear it. If you want to reach an Auditory, focus on your tone: steady, confident, conversational.

Kinaesthetic communicators feel their way through everything. Their pace is slower, their gestures are grounded, and they often pause before responding. They'll say things like:

'It just doesn't *feel* right.'

'I need to get a *feel* for how that would work.'

In a team setting, they're the glue—calm, practical and rational. In the paddock, they want to *touch the crop, walk the soil* and sense what's happening. They don't care about perfect slides; they care about trust and tone. If you want to connect with a Kinaesthetic, slow down, soften your voice, and give them time.

Audio Digital communicators need the logic to line up. They're the ones asking for the data, the spreadsheets, the 'how' and 'why'. You'll hear phrases like:

'Does that make *sense*?'

'What's the *structure* here?'

They think in frameworks and facts—and if you skip the details, you lose them. In ag, they're often the merch managers, R&D teams or accountants. They'll read every line of your email—twice—and they'll only commit once the maths adds up. To reach an Audio Digital, be concise, rational and prepared.

When you start noticing these styles, it's like someone's switched the paddock lights on. You see why some conversations click and others crash. You realise your best meetings aren't about *saying* more—they're about *matching* more.

It reminds me of something Troy Williams, former CEO of the National Farmers' Federation, said on the *Selling in the Paddock* podcast:

> *'Good communicators don't dominate the conversation—they direct it gently.'*

That's the skill. You don't bulldoze your way through a discussion; you *guide* it, matching how the other person processes the world. When you get that right, even tough conversations start to feel easy.

Flexing your style

Once I could spot the different communication styles, the real challenge began. *Could I flex to them in real time?*

At first, it felt awkward—like learning to drive a manual again after years in an automatic. But once you get the hang of it, you start shifting gears without even thinking.

One week, I'd be in a paddock with a Visual grower. He barely said a word—just squinted at the leaves, hands on hips, scanning everything. I started talking about canopy shape and leaf colour, then pulled out a few photos from other trial blocks. That's when his whole face changed—suddenly he was engaged, asking questions, seeing it for himself.

The next day, I was on the phone with an Auditory merch manager. We talked for nearly forty minutes—barely about product. He needed to talk about what was happening in his region, in his team, among his growers. Once he'd verbalised it all, he sighed and said, 'You know what? Let's give your mix a go this season.' It wasn't the pitch that won him over—it was the *conversation*.

Then there was the Kinaesthetic grower in Gippsland—the one who always started our visits with, 'Cuppa first?' He didn't want data or photos. He wanted to sit, talk about the season, feel comfortable. We'd walk the paddock after—side by side, no clipboard, no rush. That's where the real business got done.

And of course, there was the Audio Digital in South Australia—sharp, methodical, questions lined up like a spreadsheet. He'd listen quietly, then ask, 'Okay, but what does the data say across three seasons? And how does that compare to the control?' Once I stopped overexplaining and just laid out the facts, he was fine. He didn't need friendship; he needed a framework.

That was the lightbulb moment:

You don't have to change who you are—you just adjust the volume on the parts of you they can hear.

As Mark Dempsey, who works closely with producers as eShepherd Business Development Manager—Australia at Gallagher Animal Management, put it on *Selling in the Paddock*:

> *'The best communicators don't simplify their message—they tailor their delivery.'*

That's it. You don't need to rewrite your story for every person. You just need to tell it in a way that makes sense to *them*. Once you learn that, conversations stop feeling like persuasion and start feeling like a partnership.

And honestly? It's a relief. You spend less time convincing people and more time connecting with them. Because when you speak their language—visually, verbally, emotionally or logically—the sale essentially takes care of itself.

The more I practised spotting and flexing to different communication styles, the easier conversations became. It wasn't about manipulating people—it was about *meeting them where they were.*

When I stopped assuming everyone processed the world like I did, my meetings went from tense to effortless. The energy changed. People leaned in instead of shutting down.

And I realised something big: Communication isn't a soft skill. It's a commercial one. Because in agriculture, the cost of misunderstanding is massive—lost time, lost trust, and sometimes lost seasons.

The best communicators aren't the loudest or the most polished. They're the most *attuned.*

REFLECTION AND ACTION

Communication isn't about changing your message. It's about changing your method. The moment you stop trying to make people understand you—and start trying to understand them—is the moment everything starts to flow. That's when conversations connect. That's when sales start to feel easy. That's when paddocks—and people—start growing together.

Before your next conversation—whether it's a sales call, team meeting, or chat with a grower—take a moment to think about who's in front of you. Ask yourself:

- What words are they using—do they *see*, *hear*, *feel* or *analyse*?
- How do they sit or stand—fast-moving, relaxed, deliberate?
- What kind of detail do they ask for—pictures, conversation, connection or proof?

Then flex.

- If they're Visual, *show* them.
- If they're Auditory, *talk* it through.
- If they're Kinaesthetic, *slow* it down.
- If they're Audio Digital, *structure* it.

It takes practice, but, once you master it, communication becomes your biggest advantage—not your biggest headache.

6

THE PSYCHOLOGY OF CONNECTION

CONNECTION COMES DOWN to psychology. The way people open up, shut down, trust, hesitate or lean in is shaped by how their brain interprets safety, rapport and intention. In agriculture, where relationships carry far more weight than transactions, understanding the psychology behind connection becomes one of your biggest advantages. This chapter explores why some conversations feel effortless while others feel tense, and how small shifts in your behaviour can create deeper, more natural connections with the people you serve.

The misread moment

I was in Noosa, technically on annual leave, but when a particular grower rang, I would always answer.

I was walking down Hastings Street, sun on my face, coffee in hand, when the call came through. The grower's name flashed up, and I smiled. He was one of my good ones—a straight shooter.

'Hey mate,' I said, cheerfully.

Except he wasn't calling for a chat. The seed I'd sent hadn't germinated the way he'd hoped. He sounded frustrated—and rightly so. This was a big crop; it mattered to his customers.

Straight away I switched from holiday mode to *fix-it mode.* I grabbed my notebook, sat on a low wall outside a boutique, and started asking questions.

Lot numbers? Tick.

Variety details? Tick.

How was it sent, stored, planted? Tick, tick, tick.

Every box, I was confident I could tick. Still, something in his voice made my stomach drop.

I called one of our crop specialists to double-check the germ on that variety. He told me it was 'pretty good', but that the line wasn't bred for Australian conditions—so slightly lower germination was expected.

That was all I needed to hear. I felt reassured. So when I rang the grower back, I slipped into a tone that felt calm and professional—but in hindsight came off as cocky.

I told him, 'We've checked everything on our end, and the germination result is actually within range.'

Silence.

Then he exploded. He absolutely *tore strips off me*. And honestly, I don't blame him. I'd checked *my* side of the fence—logistics, germ tests, certificates.

But I hadn't stopped to think about *his*. From his side, this wasn't a technical issue—it was a business problem. A reputation problem.

His customers were depending on those plants. He'd made promises based on the seed I'd supplied, and now he was the one wearing the fallout. And instead of empathy, I'd given him evidence.

He told me he wanted to see my boss—and he wasn't mucking around. I'll admit, I was rattled. I'd never had a customer speak to me like that before. Thankfully, two weeks later my boss had my back. He flew down to Tasmania, and together we visited the property.

When we got there, we walked the crop—thin in patches, healthy in others. My boss didn't rush. He looked, listened and finally said, 'What do you need from us? How can we fix this?' The grower didn't hesitate. 'Seed,' he said. 'I just need more seed to fill the holes.'

It was that simple. We were a seed company. We had seed. The solution had been sitting right there all along—I just hadn't *heard* it. If I'd listened properly, if I'd shown even a fraction of the compassion my boss did in that moment, it never would've escalated.

That day taught me one of the biggest lessons of my career: Empathy doesn't weaken you in sales. It anchors you.

What I learnt about emotion in sales

Looking back, I can see exactly what went wrong that day in Noosa. I'd handled the facts but not the feelings. I'd treated the call like a technical problem when it was really an emotional one.

The seed was just the symptom. The real issue was *trust*. The grower wasn't angry about germination—he was angry because I didn't *get it*. He needed me to see the ripple effect—the customers he'd have to call, the hours he'd lose replanting, the doubt it would sow in his own business relationships. And instead of meeting him there, I went straight to logic.

That's the funny thing about sales. We spend so much time learning to handle objections that we forget every objection has an emotion underneath it.

That grower wasn't looking for data—he was looking for reassurance. He wanted someone to *stand beside him*, not stand over him with a clipboard. In DISC terms, he was a classic high D/C—driven, direct, detail-oriented. He needed clarity, confidence and control. And I was a high I—energetic, optimistic, eager to smooth things over. We were speaking different emotional dialects.

When I said, 'The germination is within range,' he heard, 'You're overreacting.' When I said, 'It's performing as expected,' he heard, 'You don't know what you're talking about.'

It wasn't arrogance—it was misalignment. He was Kinaesthetic—he needed to *see action, feel supported and sense that I cared*. I was stuck in Audio Digital mode—explaining logic and process, ticking boxes. So while I was delivering information, he was craving *connection*.

It reminded me of something Jimmy Blain said on *Selling in the Paddock*:

> *'People remember how you made them feel long after they forget what you said.'*

That day, I made a grower feel dismissed—even though that was never my intention. It took months to rebuild the relationship. I went back several times that season, not just talking product, but rebuilding trust. Eventually the tension softened, and now our relationship is stronger than it ever was before. Because nothing builds trust faster than owning it when you've got it wrong—and choosing to *feel* before you *fix*.

Seeing through their eyes

That trip changed the way I handled every tough conversation after that. Before then, I thought being professional meant staying calm, rational and composed—keeping emotion out of it. Now I know that staying human *is* being professional.

When things go wrong—and in agriculture, they will—people don't just want answers—they want *understanding.* So instead of rushing to defend my point, I started to ask more questions.

'What's happening on your end?'

'How's this affecting things for you?'

'What do you need from me to make it right?'

I learnt that sometimes the best thing you can do isn't to solve the problem—it's to *stand next to the person who's living it.* Because when you make someone feel heard, the tension drops. The conversation softens. Solutions appear.

I remember walking into another grower's shed not long after that. He had an issue with crop performance too—but this time, I didn't go in armed with test results. I went in with empathy. We walked the rows together. I asked questions and didn't interrupt. By the end of that walk, he wasn't angry any more. He was relieved. Because what he really needed wasn't another technical answer—he needed someone to *see it through his eyes.* That's when I started to understand what real emotional intelligence looks like in agriculture.

It reminded me of something Paul Roos said on *Selling in the Paddock*:

> *'The best leaders aren't the ones who never get emotional—they're the ones who know what to do with emotion when it shows up.'*

That's what the Tassie grower needed from me. He didn't need calm detachment—he needed *emotional leadership.* To acknowledge his frustration without taking it personally. To show care without collapsing under the pressure. To lead with steadiness, not smoothness. And that's what empathy does—it gives you the steadiness to hold space for someone else's storm.

Holding your ground and holding space

That day in Tasmania, standing in that patchy crop beside my boss and the grower, taught me more about sales than any workshop ever could. It wasn't a lesson about product or process. It was about *people*. It showed me that when something goes wrong, our first instinct is usually to defend ourselves—to explain, justify, prove we've done nothing wrong. But when we do that, we stop listening. The real skill is holding your ground *and* holding space for someone else's emotion at the same time. That's not weakness—that's strength.

When I spoke with Mark Rizkalla, a negotiation specialist from Scotwork Australia, he explained it in a way that stayed with me. Mark has coached leaders and sales teams across the country on how to negotiate under pressure, and his perspective cuts through the noise:

> *'Most people think negotiation is about being clever with words. But it's really about recognising emotion—yours and theirs—and finding a way to trade value instead of tension.'*

That's exactly what my boss did that day. He didn't push back or try to win the argument. He simply asked, 'What do you need from us? How can we fix this?' It wasn't about being right; it was about being real. And that's what connection in sales really is—the ability to step out of your own perspective and see the world through someone else's.

REFLECTION AND ACTION

Empathy doesn't slow down business. It saves it. When you lead with empathy—in sales, in teams, in life—you don't just fix problems. You build trust that lasts. Because when you choose to *feel before you fix*, everything changes. The customer stops seeing you as the company—they start seei-ng you as a partner. And that's when relationships become stronger than the setbacks. Before your next challenging conversation, pause for a moment. Ask yourself:

- Am I trying to prove I'm right or to understand what's wrong?
- What might this person be feeling beneath the words?
- What does 'fixing it' look like from their side of the fence?
- Have I earned the right to speak, or do I still need to listen?

PART 3

HANDLE THE HARD BITS

BY NOW, YOU'VE probably realised something. Sales—and leadership—aren't just about skill. They're about people.

In Part 2, we looked at connection—how to read others, build trust, and flex your communication so your message actually lands. But here's the truth most people avoid talking about: Even when you get all of that right, things can still go sideways.

You'll get pushback. You'll lose a deal that should've been yours. You'll be blamed for things that weren't your fault. And you'll have days where you wonder if it's even worth it. That's the part no one puts on the brochure. But it's also where the real growth happens. Influence isn't tested when things are easy—it's revealed when they're not.

Part 3 is about those moments. The tough calls, the hard conversations, and the situations that make your stomach drop. It's about handling pressure without losing your integrity, and staying steady when the paddock gets muddy. Let me give you a real-life example.

Failure is not an option

In April 1970, NASA launched Apollo 13—the third mission intended to land on the Moon. Fifty-six hours in, an oxygen tank exploded, crippling the spacecraft and turning a dream mission into a fight for survival. Three astronauts were suddenly trapped more than 300,000 kilometres from Earth with dwindling oxygen, limited power, and systems failing one by one.

Flight director Gene Kranz gathered his team at Mission Control and said five words that would define not just that mission, but generations of leadership that followed:

> *'Failure is not an option.'*

What followed wasn't luck—it was *calm under chaos*. A room full of engineers stopped panicking and started problem-solving. They stripped the problem down to what they *did* have: duct tape, checklists, human brains and a deadline.

They improvised a carbon-dioxide filter out of spare parts. They rerouted power manually. They recalculated entry angles with pencils and slide rules. The entire world watched, but the team kept its focus small—one problem at a time.

And when Apollo 13 finally splashed down safely, the moment wasn't just a triumph of technology. It was proof of what happens when people keep their heads and hearts steady under pressure.

What this means for ag sales

In agriculture, we might not be floating in space, but we've all had our own Apollo 13 moments.

The year when the crop failed.

When the market collapsed.

When you thought, *This might be it.*

In those moments, you can't afford panic—you need perspective. You can't control everything that breaks, but you can control your response. Because leadership—whether in space or in the paddock—is often about solving one problem at a time when everything feels impossible.

KEY TAKEAWAY

Part 3 is not about pretending things don't go wrong. It's about learning how to breathe, refocus and lead through the breakdown.

So let's start small—with the everyday 'explosions' of sales life—the objections, the pushback, the moments that test your calm and character. Because if Apollo 13 taught us anything, it's this: When pressure hits, composure is the real oxygen.

7

HANDLING CUSTOMER OBJECTIONS WITH THE 3 CS

EVERY SALESPERSON, NO matter how skilled or experienced, will face objections. They're a normal, healthy part of the decision-making process—not a sign that the conversation is failing. The real challenge isn't the objection itself; it's how you respond. This chapter is about approaching objections with calm, clarity and confidence (the three Cs), so you can keep the conversation open instead of shutting it down. When you learn to stay steady, listen fully and address concerns without defensiveness, objections stop feeling personal and start becoming opportunities to build trust, deepen understanding and move the relationship forward.

'That's too expensive'

I've heard those three words more times than I can count.

Sometimes they come with a chuckle, sometimes a challenge, and sometimes with that long silence that makes you want to fill the gap with a discount.

Early in my career, that phrase used to rattle me. I'd instantly start justifying—listing trial data, yield improvements, shelf life, colour retention—anything to prove the price was worth it. But here's what I eventually learnt: Most of the time, *price isn't the problem*.

When someone says, 'It's too expensive,' they're really saying one of three things:

- 'I don't see the value yet.'
- 'I've been burnt before.'
- 'I don't know if I can trust you.'

The words are about money; the emotion underneath is about *risk*.

A few years back at a field day in Gippsland—on a chilly, wind-bitten morning—everyone was huddled over paper cups of coffee. A grower I knew well walked up, eyed the trial plot, and said, 'Looks good, Georgia. But bloody hell, that seed's dear. Can you sharpen the pencil a bit?'

Old me would've jumped straight to defence mode. Instead, I paused.

'Yeah, it is on the higher side,' I said. 'What are you comparing it to?'

He shrugged. 'The usual—the one I've used for the last five years.'

I asked a few more questions. Turned out he wasn't just comparing *price*. He was comparing *security*. That seed had never let him down. It was predictable. He knew how it performed in his soil, his weather, his system.

So when he said 'expensive', what he meant was, 'I'm not sure it's worth the risk of change.'

That changed everything. I stopped talking numbers and started talking *value*. I showed him how the crop held its colour longer—fewer sprays, fewer labour hours, better quality at harvest. We worked out what that meant in his real costs per hectare.

I could see the shift happen—his shoulders dropped, his eyes narrowed, calculating. He didn't order that day. But he rang a week later and said, 'All right, let's give it a go on one paddock.' That's the thing about objections. They're not rejections—they're *requests for reassurance.*

It reminded me of something Mark Rizkalla said on *Selling in the Paddock*:

> *'Negotiation isn't about pushing harder—it's about understanding what the other side truly values.'*

Exactly. When someone pushes back on price, don't rush to defend. Get curious. Find out what *value* looks like to them—not to you. Because once you know that, you're no longer negotiating against each other; you're negotiating *with* each other.

Price is the easiest objection to say out loud—but it's rarely the deepest one. The tougher objections are quieter, and they're the ones that come from experience and disappointment. The next one usually sounds like this: 'I've tried something like this before… and it didn't work.' Let's go there.

'I've been burnt before'

This is rarely said with anger—more often it comes out slow, like someone flexing a joint that's still sore. There's a pause, a shift in body language—arms fold tighter, shoulders close in—like they're guarding a wound that hasn't fully healed. You can *feel* it before you even hear it. The hesitation. The caution. That silent, 'Don't touch that—it still hurts.'

In ag, being 'burnt' isn't just about a bad product—it's about *broken trust*. It's the scorch mark left behind when someone believed a promise and got let down. It's the ache between what was said and what actually happened.

Maybe it was a supplier who overpromised and underdelivered. Maybe it was a rep who disappeared after the sale. Maybe it was a product that looked perfect in the brochure but flopped in the field. Whatever the story, the bruise is still there—tender, but mending. And the hardest part? You're not just selling a new product—you're asking them to risk disappointment *again*.

I remember sitting in a farm ute with a grower who said those exact words. He'd trialled a product from another company the year before. It looked brilliant on paper—high yield promise, clean canopy, strong data. But in the paddock it was patchy germination, uneven growth, and a rep who stopped answering calls once the invoice was paid.

So when I turned up with something similar, he folded his arms across his chest, leaning back into the seat, eyes fixed on the windscreen.

'Not doing that again, Georgia. Got burnt last time.'

Fair enough.

I could've launched into how my product was different—new genetics, new backing—but I didn't. 'Yeah, I get that,' I said. 'I've been on the other side of that too—chasing someone down for answers.'

He looked over then—not convinced yet, but curious. His shoulders eased a little.

'Yeah,' he said quietly. 'Well . . . you remember who shows up.'

That line stuck with me. Because that's all he wanted—*someone to show up*.

It reminded me of something Justin Haydock shared on the *Selling in the Paddock* podcast. Justin is a wool sales professional with West Coast Wools, and he understands the dynamics of small, tight-knit regional communities better than most. He said:

> *'In small communities, trust isn't built through promises—it's built through presence.'*

And he's right.

The longer I work in ag, the clearer it becomes: People don't want perfect reps. They want *reliable* ones. They want the person who answers the phone when things go wrong, who'll stand in the paddock and look them in the eye, and who'll own it—even when it's uncomfortable.

That's how you handle the 'I've been burnt before' objection—not with logic, but with consistency. You don't argue about their past. You acknowledge it. You show up, again and again, until they start to believe that *you're not the same story*. Because when someone says, 'I've been burnt before', what they're really saying is, 'Prove to me this time will be different.' And that takes time, not talk.

The next objection usually comes from a different place—not pain, but loyalty. It sounds like: 'I already have a supplier.' That's not a wall; it's a compliment. They're telling you they value trust. So how do you honour that loyalty without walking away from the conversation? Let's talk about that next.

'I already have a supplier'

There's a certain way people say it—friendly but firm. It's not defensive. It's protective. Like a gate that's been closed for good reason.

I've learnt to take that as a compliment. It means they value loyalty. And in ag, loyalty isn't just business—it's personal.

Most growers stick with people who've stood beside them in the tough seasons—through late deliveries, weather wipe-outs, and those years when everything that could go wrong did. You can *feel* the weight of that loyalty—like a well-worn pair of boots. Comfortable. Reliable. Proven. So when someone says, 'I already have a supplier,' what they're really saying is, 'This person has earned my trust. And you haven't—yet.'

I remember standing in a spinach paddock in Gippsland—cold wind cutting across the leaves, the ground still damp from overnight rain. A grower I hadn't met before walked me through the rows, proud as anything.

'This one's a ripper,' he said, pointing to a variety that was standing tall, dark green, tough as nails. 'Been using it for years. Never lets me down.'

He wasn't trying to shut me down; he was showing me his *proof*.

I nodded. 'Looks great,' I said. 'What made you pick this one originally?'

He told me the story—a trial that worked, a rep who had his back, a time the company replaced seed without question. As he spoke, I could hear the trust in his voice. I didn't try to sell over the top of that. I respected it.

Then I said, 'Sounds like you've got a good partnership there. If you ever want to see what else is coming through the pipeline, I'd love to show you—no strings, just options.'

He looked at me for a second, weighing me up—not just what I'd said, but *how* I'd said it.

Then he smiled. 'Yeah, all right. Keep me in the loop.'

That's it. Door cracked. You don't break loyalty by pushing harder. You earn respect by showing it first. Because one day—and it always happens—something will go wrong. A variety won't perform. A rep will move on. A delivery will miss its window. And when that happens, the grower will think back to the people who were professional, kind and confident enough to respect the boundary without trying to climb over it. That's your moment.

It reminds me of something Andrew Morgan shared on the *Selling in the Paddock* podcast. Andrew is the managing director of SFM—a future-focused forestry company—and co-founder of Hydrowood, one of the most innovative timber recovery projects in Australia. He has a deep understanding of long-term relationships in primary industries, and his insight captures it beautifully:

> '*Strong relationships are built in the quiet seasons. That's when people decide who they'll trust when the next storm hits.*'

Exactly. The best reps aren't fighting for today's business—they're positioning for tomorrow's trust. So when you hear, 'I already have a supplier,' smile and mean it. Because what they're really telling you is what matters most to them. And that's the key to every future sale.

This next one's the hardest—because it's the most honest. It's not hidden behind price or loyalty; it's said right to your face. 'Why should I trust you?' Let's talk about that—and what it really takes to answer it.

'Why should I trust you?'

Every now and then, someone cuts through all the polite talk and just asks this outright. No softening. No smile. Just truth, sitting heavy in the air.

The first time I heard it, it stopped me cold. We were standing beside a shed in Tassie, wind snapping the tin, dust lifting from the track. The grower's arms were crossed, his boots planted firm. I could tell this wasn't about me—not really. It was about every rep before me who'd made a promise and vanished.

My instinct was to rush in and defend myself—list experience, trials, results. But then I remembered the Apollo 13 lesson: When everything's tense, the worst thing you can do is panic. So I took a breath.

'I don't expect you to trust me yet,' I said. 'That's something I'll have to earn.'

He didn't move. I didn't fill the silence. We just stood there for a moment—two people, one question hanging between us.

Finally, he said, 'All right. We'll see.'

And that was the beginning. Not of a sale—of trust. Trust in ag doesn't arrive wrapped in a signature or an order form. It arrives slowly—like rain after a long dry. At first it's a drizzle. Then a steady fall. Then one day you look up, and everything's growing again.

You can't talk someone into trusting you. You show them. You show up when it's uncomfortable, when there's nothing to sell, when the season turns against you. You prove you'll keep showing up even when there's no spotlight, no commission, no easy win. That's what trust sounds like. Not promises—footsteps.

It reminds me of something Justin Haydock said on *Selling in the Paddock*:

> *'People don't need you to be perfect. They just need to know you'll be there when it counts.'*

That's the truth behind every objection. They're all just ways of asking, 'Can I count on you when it matters?' And the answer isn't found in your pitch deck. It's found in your behaviour. That's how you build credibility in the paddock—not by pushing harder, but by standing steadier.

REFLECTION AND ACTION

In sales, as in space, calm is the real oxygen. And trust—just like survival—depends on how well you breathe under pressure.

When the next objection comes—and it will—try this:

- Breathe before you answer.
- Listen with your eyes, not just your ears. Notice what's behind the words.
- Acknowledge the emotion first. Logic can wait.
- Be steady. Your calm is their reassurance.

8

WHEN THE SEASON TURNS

EVERY CAREER IN agriculture has a turning point—a moment where the season shifts, the ground changes beneath you and something you thought was solid suddenly isn't. Sometimes it's a crop, a customer, a trial, a team. Sometimes it's you.

In ag, the season never just turns on the outside. It turns on the inside too. The pressure. The disappointment. The grief no one talks about. The resilience you didn't know you had until the moment demanded it.

This chapter is about those times—the hard seasons, the human seasons, and the quiet courage required to start again. Because every rep, every grower, every leader learns this truth eventually:

You don't get to control the season—only how you show up when it turns.

The season that broke the trial

Early in my career, I sowed a rocket trial out in Clyde. I'd done everything right—textbook spacing, clean emergence, uniform growth. Four weeks later, it looked like a photo you'd put in a brochure.

Then week five arrived. The wind picked up, dragging light sandy soil with it until it turned the paddock into a sand-blaster. By the next morning, my perfect trial was shredded. Leaves torn. Rows wiped. Months of planning gone in a single night.

The grower walked up beside me, hands in pockets.

'Bugger,' he said. 'Happens.'

He was steady. I was gutted. It wasn't about pride—it was about time. A whole season of data wiped out. A story we'd have to retell in twelve months, not twelve days.

Standing there in the grit and silence, I realised something important: **Nature doesn't apologise. And it doesn't care about your spreadsheet**.

But it did teach me something. That day we decided every key trial would be duplicated somewhere else. One to learn from. One to lean on.

Control isn't about certainty—it's about preparation. And sometimes preparation is all you can take into the next season.

Holding steady when everyone's watching

There's a particular quiet that falls when something you're responsible for hasn't performed. You can feel it before anyone speaks—folded arms, slow nods, the subtle glance that says, 'Is this it?'

I felt that once while walking a group through a demonstration block that simply hadn't hit its mark. Late sowing, cold snap, pests—a cocktail of undesirable factors.

My instinct was to defend myself. My next instinct was to hide. But then I remembered something I'd learnt the hard way: **Your credibility is built in the moments you don't flinch.**

So I told the truth.

'This one hasn't performed the way we hoped. Here's why... and here's what it's taught us.'

The energy shifted immediately. Shoulders unclenched. Questions flowed. A few growers stayed back to chat through next steps.

That's the thing people forget: **You don't build trust by being perfect. You build it by being honest**.

James Grafas is a professional director, founder of James People, co-founder of Good Trust and a chartered member of the Institute of Directors. He works closely with boards, leaders and organisations navigating growth, transition and governance—where trust, clarity and capability matter more than control. James has spent his career helping leaders build others up rather than hold them tight, and his perspective cuts through one of the most common leadership traps: mistaking control for competence. James said something profound when he came on the podcast:

'People trust calm more than perfection.'

And that's the real test when the season turns. Not whether you got everything right. But whether you remained steady when you *didn't* get everything right.

Reframing failure as feedback

For a long time, failure felt personal. If a trial went sideways, if a block didn't perform, if a season tanked—I'd replay every decision, looking for the one wrong step.

But over time, I realised something: **Failure isn't a verdict. It's data**.

Andrew Morgan summed it up perfectly on the podcast:

'Pressure doesn't destroy systems; it reveals the gaps.'

So instead of beating myself up, I started asking better questions:

Where did the process break?
What assumptions were wrong?
How do we build a buffer next time?

We added debriefs, mid-season checks and backup sites. Small things that came from big lessons.

Celia Leverton is chair of the Regenerative Agriculture Network Tasmania, a farmer, grazing consultant, permaculture designer and teacher. She works at the intersection of land, people and systems, helping farmers and communities adapt to change rather than resist it. Celia spends her days observing how natural systems respond under pressure—drought, degradation, transition—and how resilience is built through adjustment, not control. Her perspective reminds us that progress in agriculture, like nature itself, isn't linear.

Celia once said something that stuck with me:

> *'Nature doesn't fail; it reorganises.'*

And so do we—if we let ourselves. Every tough season leaves compost behind. Messy, painful... but rich with insight. You either use it or you waste it.

Grief and loss, in hearts and paddocks

Grief in agriculture is constant—and mostly silent. It's the grief of a crop ploughed in after months of care. The grief of livestock lost. The grief of waste, of weather, of all the unseen effort no one claps for.

And then there's the human grief. I'll never forget the grower who rang me one morning for seed. Halfway through the conversation, she took a breath and said quietly, 'George passed away last week.'

Her husband. Her partner. Her life. There was nothing clever to offer. No neat sentence to fix anything. So I just stayed on the line. We cried together. We remembered stories. We let the silence be what it needed to be. She didn't need a rep that day. She needed presence.

That's grief in ag—not loud, not dramatic. Just present. Just heavy. Just real.

Loss doesn't always come from people. Sometimes it comes from the land. Floodwater taking a hundred head of cattle in one night. Hail flattening spinach two days before harvest. A truckload of produce rejected for being half a shade the wrong colour.

You can hear grief in the simple sentences growers use:

'They were good animals.'
'We'll plough it in.'
'It just wasn't the year.'

It's dignity in heartbreak. Strength without show. Resilience without applause. And while the world moves on, the people in agriculture quietly absorb the hit, reset and start again.

People in ag are conditioned to 'get on with it'. Work through it. Push through it. Say nothing. But unspoken grief is like salt under a paddock—invisible yet corrosive.

Celia is right: Regeneration isn't just about soil. It's about people too. Naming a loss doesn't make you weak. It makes you honest. You can't lead well—or sell well—if you're still carrying yesterday's heartbreak in your chest. Sometimes the bravest thing you can do is acknowledge it. Sometimes it's acknowledging it for someone else.

Starting again

Recovery in ag is rarely dramatic. It's quiet. It's standing in a new paddock after a hard season, watching fresh shoots break through soil you'd sworn was finished. It's walking back into the paddock that hurt you, realising you're no longer scared of it. It's seeing the season turn—outside and inside—and trusting yourself enough to start again.

When the Apollo 13 mission went wrong, the crew didn't have time to panic. Neither do we. You breathe. You focus. You solve one problem at a time.

There's a line I wrote in my notebook after that Clyde trial: **Don't fight the wind—learn to work with it**.

That's what starting again really is. Not erasing the past. Integrating it.

REFLECTION AND ACTION

Seasons always turn. The question is not *if* or *when* they turn but *how you meet them when they do*. And every time you meet a new season, good or bad, with steadiness, honesty, empathy and resilience, you grow something far more powerful than a product or a paddock. You grow yourself.

Think about your last tough season—in work or in life.

- What did it show you about yourself?
- What did it strip back?
- What did it strengthen?
- What did you lose?
- What did you learn?
- What might you do differently next time?
- And who stood beside you when everything tilted?

Write it down. Name it. Honour it.

9

LEGACY AND LEADERSHIP

AFTER THE HARD SEASONS, something shifts. You start to think about the people who taught you, the ones who steadied you, and the lessons that shaped who you've become in the paddock and beyond it.

That's where legacy begins—not at the end of a career, but in the moments where you choose how to lead. This chapter is about those choices, and the leadership that lasts long after you've driven out of the driveway.

Carrying forward what matters

Legacy isn't about keeping everything the same. It's about carrying forward what matters most. In agriculture, legacy is everywhere—in the soil, the seed, the systems and the stories.

You can feel it when you walk onto a property that's been farmed by the same family for generations. There's a rhythm, a history that hums beneath every decision. But legacy can be heavy, too. It's the expectation to keep things going exactly as they are. To honour those who came before while also steering towards what's next.

I've sat at plenty of kitchen tables where that tension sits thick in the air—the older generation holding on, the younger one holding back, both wanting the same thing but speaking different languages.

One side says, 'Don't change what's worked.'

The other says, 'Let me try something new.'

The truth is, both are right. And the best leaders are the ones who find the middle ground—the space where history and innovation can sit side by side.

When I spoke with Californian farmer Jason Giannelli, from R&G Fanucchi and Old River Farming Company, on *Selling in the Paddock*, he said something that summed it up perfectly:

> *'Respect for what's been built doesn't mean resistance to change.'*

Legacy leadership isn't about rewriting the past; it's about expanding it. It's about knowing when to protect a principle and when to evolve a process. It's about remembering that the goal isn't to be the same as those before you—it's to be worthy of what they built.

Lessons that outlive us

When I think about legacy, I think about the people who taught me how to lead—sometimes without even meaning to.

The grower who said, 'We've all been there,' when my trial went sideways. The manager who stood beside me in that Tasmanian paddock and asked the simplest, most powerful question: 'What do you need from us?' The woman who kept farming after her husband passed away, because it's what he would've wanted.

None of them left me manuals or spreadsheets. They left me *moments*. And those moments turned into lessons that outlive all of us.

Legacy isn't always a grand gesture or a family name carved into a gatepost. Sometimes it's the small things—the words people hear when you're not around. The way they remember how you made them feel. That's what leadership in ag really is—a living legacy built one conversation, one decision, one season at a time.

The next generation

Every leader I know in agriculture has one eye on the future—not just on next season, but on who's coming up behind them. And yet, one of the hardest things to do is *let go*. To step aside and let someone else drive. To trust that the next generation will do things differently—and that 'different' doesn't mean 'wrong'.

I remember chatting with James Grafas about succession and culture in ag. He said:

> *'Our job isn't to hand over control—it's to hand over confidence.'*

That line stopped me in my tracks. Because that's it, isn't it? Legacy leadership isn't about micromanaging the future. It's about teaching people to think, decide and lead on their own. It's mentoring instead of managing. Guiding instead of guarding. And trusting that your influence will last longer than your presence.

Faith in what you've built

I often think about the grower who lost her partner and kept showing up. Every season she plants is an act of remembrance.

Every paddock she tends is a promise kept. That's what legacy looks like. Not a monument—a continuation.

When people ask me what good leadership in agriculture looks like, I think of those moments—quiet strength, humble persistence, courage through heartbreak. It's not the awards or the yield charts. It's the ability to keep building something that matters, long after the people who started it are gone.

It reminds me of something Andrew Morgan said:

> *'Real leaders plant trees they'll never sit under.'*

That's what Part 3 has been about—learning to handle the hard bits, to sit with loss and pressure and imperfection, and to lead anyway. Legacy isn't about holding on. It's about letting go—gracefully, confidently, and with faith that what you've built will continue to grow.

REFLECTION AND ACTION

Legacy isn't a story about the past. It's a blueprint for how we move forward. And in ag, where everything begins and ends with the seasons, maybe the most powerful thing we can do is make sure what we plant—in soil, in people, in ourselves—keeps growing long after we're gone.

Think about the people who've shaped you—the ones whose lessons you still carry.

- What did they leave behind that mattered most?
- What do you want to leave behind when it's your turn?

It might not be a business or a name. It might just be a way of being—calm under pressure, kind in conflict, honest when it counts.

PART 4

DRIVE IT HOME

YOU'VE BUILT the connection. You've asked the questions. You've listened, learnt, and led the conversation with intent. Now comes the moment most people avoid—the moment where the relationship meets reality.

Closing.

Closing isn't pressure. It isn't manipulation. It's clarity. It's guiding someone towards a decision that serves them—and having the courage to ask for it.

Most reps stumble here not because they lack skill, but because they hesitate. They soften. They hope the customer will magically close themselves. But influence doesn't work like that. Leadership doesn't work like that. Sales definitely doesn't work like that.

This part of the book is about the shift from 'I hope' to 'I lead'. From circling the point to landing it. From good conversations to confident conversions.

Here, we turn courage into action. We look at the language, the timing, the mindset and the presence required to ask for what you've earned—and receive it. Because closing isn't the end of the relationship. It's the beginning of the next season. And if you've done the work well, asking isn't scary. It's the most natural step in the world. Before we delve in, let me share one final real-life example.

Don't mumble the close

Ted Sorensen, John F. Kennedy's legendary speechwriter, once said that clarity is the highest form of respect you can give an audience. He believed words were tools for action—and that every sentence should move people closer to a decision.

Years later, Sorensen told a story that became folklore among communicators. He was working with a man on death row who was preparing for his final appeal. The man had spent hours writing and rewriting his statement—pouring his heart into it—but when the time came to deliver it, he mumbled. His voice shook, his eyes dropped and his words lost their force.

Afterwards, Sorensen said quietly, 'If there was ever a time to speak clearly, this was it.'

That line stayed with me. Because it's not just about speeches or politics. It's about *life*. Every day, we all have moments that matter—moments to ask, to lead, to close. Moments when mumbling costs us connection, clarity or opportunity.

What this means for ag sales

In agriculture—and in sales—'mumbling the close' looks different. It's when you've built trust, run the trial, proven the value... and then soften the ask. It's when you say, 'Maybe we could look at it next season,' instead of, 'Would you like to order some for next season?' It's when you circle around commitment because you don't want to feel pushy, forgetting that confidence isn't arrogance—it's service. Because if you truly believe in what you're offering, you *owe it* to your customer to be clear.

I've done it myself. I've built rapport, nailed the presentation, felt the energy in the room . . . and then tiptoed around the final step.

It usually sounds like: 'So . . . what are your thoughts?' What I meant was: 'Let's do this.'

But I was afraid to say it. Afraid of rejection. Afraid of seeming too forward. And every time I've done that, I've felt that sinking feeling on the drive home—knowing I'd let fear mumble when courage should've spoken.

KEY TAKEAWAY

You don't need to be loud to be clear. You just need to be *committed*. Because clarity isn't pressure—it's professionalism.

As Mark Rizkalla said on *Selling in the Paddock*:

> *'In negotiation, hesitation costs you power. Clarity earns you respect.'*

And it's true. The close isn't about forcing a yes—it's about giving people the confidence to decide. When you're clear, you serve. When you mumble, you steal the chance for clarity—from yourself and from them.

So whether you're selling seed, leading a team, or having a hard conversation, remember Sorensen's death row story. This is your moment. Speak clearly. Ask directly. Don't mumble the close. Because courage unspoken is just potential. And potential doesn't change the world—action does.

10

THE CLOSING TOOLKIT

YOU'VE ALREADY BUILT the relationship. You've asked the questions. You've uncovered the need. Now it's about landing the conversation with simple, honest language that helps your customer make a decision.

This chapter is your closing toolkit—the questions, cues, mindset shifts and practical scripts that take you from a good conversation to a committed next step. Because closing isn't about pressure. It's about direction. And when you know what to say and how to say it, asking becomes the easiest part of the job.

Closing transforms interest into action

Every grower, every customer, every buyer is busy. They've got animals to feed, crops to manage, people to lead, bills to pay, weather to watch—and they are constantly triaging what gets attention.

A conversation with you is one moment in a jam-packed day. That's why clarity matters so much. If you don't close the loop, their attention moves on—not because they're rejecting you, but because life in ag is loud.

Most reps don't fail at closing because they don't know what to say. They fail because they **never actually say it**. They circle. They repeat themselves. They wait for the customer to 'give them a sign'. They soften the ask to avoid discomfort. But a conversation without a clear next step isn't influence—it's just chat. Closing is what transforms interest into action.

The closing mindset

One shift instantly makes closing easier: **You're not taking anything from them—you're guiding them to what they've already said they want.**

You've listened. You've understood. You've connected the dots. You've found a solution that fits.

Closing is simply the moment when you help them take the next logical step. There's no manipulation, no pressure, no tricks. Just leadership. Closing well requires three things:

1. **Permission**. Not 'Can I?' permission—emotional permission. The trust you've earned by showing you care.
2. **Clarity**. Simple, direct language. No fluff. No overexplaining.
3. **Courage**. Not loud courage—steady courage. The kind that says, 'I'm confident in the value of this conversation.'

When you approach closing with leadership instead of fear, everything relaxes—both for you and for the customer.

The conversation prompts that convert

Here are the practical prompts, phrases and questions that keep you clear, grounded and effective—especially when your nerves want to take over.

The commitment close

Use when the customer is clear and on board.

- 'Shall we go ahead with this?'
- 'Would you like me to lock this in?'
- 'What's the next step on your end to get this started?'

Simple. Direct. No BS.

The trial close

This helps you check their temperature without pressure.

- 'How does this feel to you so far?'
- 'Does this look like it would solve the issue you mentioned?'
- 'Is there anything here that doesn't quite fit?'

If they hesitate, you stay curious—not pushy.

The action close

Perfect for agriculture, where people are used to planning around seasons and windows. Action creates momentum.

- 'When would you like this in the ground?'
- 'When do you want product on-farm?'
- 'What timing suits your program best?'

The calendar close

Gets the decision out of the air and into real time.

- 'Would you prefer delivery this week or next?'
- 'Should we walk this in before or after the rain clears?'
- 'Do you want to start the trial now, or wait until the next planting window?'

The two-option close

Not pushy—it just gives direction. Humans choose more easily when guided.

- 'Do you want the standard program or the premium?'
- 'Do you want to start with ten hectares or the full block?'
- 'Would you like one load or two?'

Handling the moment

A close will fall apart only three ways:

1. **Your voice gets shaky**. Solution: Breathe once, and slow down your first sentence.
2. **You waffle**. Solution: Ask the question, then shut up.
3. **You overexplain**. Solution: Trust what you've already said.

The close should sound like something you'd say in a normal conversation. Think: honest, human, steady. Your tone matters more than your words. If you sound calm and clear, your customer feels calm and clear. Closing is not about convincing. It's about confirming.

If they say 'I need to think about it'

This is where most reps fall apart—or give up. Don't. Curiosity is your friend. Ask:

- 'No worries at all—what part do you want to think over?'
- 'What's the main hesitation for you?'
- 'Is it timing, price, value or something else?'

You're not poking. You're clarifying. And nine times out of ten, the thing they 'need to think about' is something easily solved with a conversation.

If they truly need more time? Give it—but put a fence around it. You could say:

- 'How about I give you a buzz on Thursday after you've had a look?'
- 'Let's check in early next week—what day suits?'

A close without a follow-up is dead in the paddock. More on this in a moment.

If they say no

A 'no' is never a personal rejection. In ag, it usually means:

- Wrong timing,
- Wrong window,
- Wrong budget,
- Wrong season,
- Wrong pressure point, or simply
- 'Not today'.

Stay gracious. Stay steady. Stay curious. You could say:

- 'No worries at all—what would need to change for this to be worth revisiting?'
- 'When would the timing be better for you?'
- 'Do you want me to keep you in the loop for the next round?'

A 'no for now' is often a 'yes' next season. Good reps treat 'no' as information. Great reps treat it as a pipeline.

The follow-through

Closing isn't the final step—it's the first step of the next relationship. After the customer says yes:

- Confirm details
- Set expectations
- Communicate next steps clearly
- Check in early
- Stay present
- Deliver on every promise

Closing earns trust. Follow-through keeps it.

REFLECTION AND ACTION

Think about your last few conversations.

Ask yourself:

- Where did you hesitate?
- Where did you soften?
- Where did you talk in circles?
- Where did you avoid the moment?
- And where did you land it?

Closing confidently takes practice—not pressure. The more you say the words out loud, the easier they become. The best closers aren't the pushiest. They're the clearest. And now, so are you.

CONCLUSION
PEOPLE IN THE PADDOCK

AGRICULTURE HAS A way of returning you to what matters. Not the products. Not the plans. Not the perfect season. But the people.

The conversations in paddocks. The trust built over years. The honesty shared over a ute tray, on a driveway or across a kitchen table. The moments when someone looks you in the eye and tells you the truth—about their season, their pressure, their hopes or their heartbreak.

If there's one thing this industry has taught me, and one thing I hope this book leaves you with, it's this: Selling in agriculture has never been about the sale. It's about the relationship that makes the sale possible.

All the tools in the world—DISC, communication styles, questioning frameworks, closing scripts—are nothing if they aren't anchored in connection. Real connection. The kind built through listening, honesty, presence and respect.

That's what makes selling in ag so different. So meaningful. So human. Because here, your reputation travels faster than your car. Your character matters more than your quota. And the way you make people feel determines whether they'll call you back when the season breaks open again.

Throughout these chapters, you've walked through the same journey every great rep and leader eventually travels:

Knowing yourself.
Understanding others.
Handling the hard bits.
Having the courage to drive it home.

You've seen how trust is built—and how quickly it can be lost. You've learnt how to stay steady when things fall apart. You've seen the grief that sits quietly in this industry, and the resilience that rises to meet it. You've discovered that leadership exists in moments—especially the small ones—and that influence comes from listening far more than talking.

And now, here at the end, we return to the beginning.

Back to the paddock

Back to the place where this work actually happens. Back to the people who make it matter.

Selling in the paddock means selling with heart. It means showing up as yourself, communicating with intention, asking better questions, and earning the right to ask for the order. It means respecting the time, the pressure, the history and the livelihood of the person standing across from you. It means remembering that behind every business, every farm, every program, every invoice—there's a human being doing their best.

And you are one of them.

You chose this work. You chose to get better at it. You chose to push yourself—in your conversations, your confidence, your courage.

For that, I'm incredibly grateful. Grateful for every person who shared their story on the *Selling in the Paddock* podcast. Grateful for the reps and leaders who let me into their world and trusted me with their challenges. Grateful for the laughter, the honesty and the deep care that runs through this industry like roots under soil.

This isn't the end. It's a beginning—a new season. A reminder that whether you're in sales, leadership, or simply trying to find your place in agriculture, your voice matters.

Keep learning. Keep connecting. Keep showing up. And when in doubt, go back to the paddock. That's where the best conversations always start.

Thank you for reading, for listening and for walking this journey with me. If you want to stay connected, join me on the *Selling in the Paddock* podcast or visit sellinginthepaddock.com to explore workshops, coaching and resources designed to help you grow your influence—one conversation at a time.

See you in the paddock.

GEORGIA STORMONT

ABOUT THE AUTHOR

GEORGIA STORMONT is an agricultural sales coach, keynote speaker, podcaster and former horticulture and dairy sales rep who has spent more than fifteen years selling in paddocks across Australia.

Through her business, Selling in the Paddock, Georgia trains and coaches agricultural sales teams to communicate with clarity, build genuine relationships, handle objections with confidence and close without feeling pushy. Her practical, human-centred approach is shaped by thousands of conversations with growers, agronomists, rural leaders and the people who keep Australian agriculture moving.

Georgia is the host of the *Selling in the Paddock* podcast—a fast-growing show known for real, grounded conversations with farmers, industry professionals and salespeople from around the world.

A passionate advocate for communication, leadership and the human side of agriculture, Georgia works with companies across the ag supply chain to build high-performing teams and develop talent at every level.

When she's not travelling for workshops or interviewing guests, you'll find her at home in Melbourne with her partner, Daniel, their three kids, and a very energetic dog named Bobby.

Continue your journey

To access tools, workshops and additional resources, visit: www.sellinginthepaddock.com

www.ingramcontent.com/pod-product-compliance
Ingram Content Group UK Ltd.
Pitfield, Milton Keynes, MK11 3LW, UK
UKHW042015190726
13854UKWH00005B/2289

9 781998 528813